This Mood Track
Journal belongs to:

_____

Contact Info:

_____

DIFFICULT ROADS OFTEN LEAD TO *beautiful* DESTINATIONS

Part One

This mood tracker journal is separated into Parts 1 and Parts 2.

Part 1 of this journal provides you with guided journal prompts & questions to write your answers and to check in with yourself daily or on a schedule you determine. Use the Sample page to give you an idea of how to use this journal.

The answers you provide each day can identify patterns. If your mood is not improving, be sure to see your physician.

Be sure to use the Positive Affirmation pages to record even more of your favorite motivational and optimistic quotes!

In Part 2, it provides you with doodle sheets & blank dot grid sheets to doodle, draw on, or write more of your thoughts. You will also find blank charts to plan your self-care goals for a healthier mind, body, and soul. In addition, there are a sampling of coloring pages that you can use when you need to de-stress from your day, which can help improve your mood, and more.

Date: *Aug. 10/19*   Wake-Up Time Today: *6 a.m.*   Hours of Sleep I Got Last Night: *7 hours*

My Mood: Morning   Afternoon   Evening

Food/Beverages I Had Today:

B   *6:30 a.m Smoothie, orange juice*

L   *2 p.m. Greek Salad, coffee*

D   *8 p.m. Crock-pot chili, milk*

Snacks   *Potato chips, carrot sticks,*

soda

What I Did for Exercise Today: **My Water Intake:**

Stairs at work

Unfortunately,

never made it to

the gym after

work. ☹

Did I feel any of the following today?:

- ☐ Sadness and/or crying
- ☐ Hopeless
- ☒ No energy/fatigue/lethargy
- ☒ Difficulty concentrating/making decisions
- ☐ Appetite is increased or decreased
- ☐ Lack of motivation
- ☐ Anger/frustration
- ☐ Lack of interest in activities normally enjoy

What caused me to feel negative emotions today?

I had a late lunch, because I was
too busy to take lunch sooner. I
was starting to get a headache by
then.

** Go to your doctor/medical professional immediately if you are suicidal or your mood is not getting better.******

SAMPLE

Is there anything that I could have done to improve my day?

I could have told my boss that I
needed to have lunch sooner so that
I could re-energize.

Positive things that happened today:

My client was thrilled with me for
the work I did to help her with her
portfolio. I had a nice
conversation with a co-worker.

Today, I am grateful for:

Having a great job.

Having my own car to drive.

My pet dog.

Goals/things I can do to make tomorrow better:

Drink more water to ward off a headache.

Then go to gym after work.

Take lunch earlier.

Get to work a bit earlier in the morning.

Positive Affirmation:

It's not selfish to do what is best for my health and
well-being.

One day at a time

My Months & Year In Color

☐ Happy, Optimistic, Positive

☐ Sad, Pessimistic, Negative

☐ Angry, Annoyed, Frustrated

☐ Anxious or Stressed

☐ Calm, Relaxed

☐

☐

Choose a color for each emotion. Then fill it in every day, and look for a pattern. Get immediate help from a medical professional if sadness, anger, or other negative emotions prevail.

There Is ALways Something to be GRATEFUL for

	J	F	M	A	M	J	J	A	S	O	N	D
1												
2												
3												
4												
5												
6												
7												
8												
9												
10												
11												
12												
13												
14												
15												
16												
17												
18												
19												
20												
21												
22												
23												
24												
25												
26												
27												
28												
29												
30												
31												

Positive Affirmation Ideas

"If you want to find happiness, find gratitude." Steve Maraboli

Everything is better when I am positive.

I respect what my body is telling me.

I look for the positive in all situations.

I find the joy in the little things in life.

My life is blessed.

I am creating the kind of life I want.

To be good to others, I first need to be good to myself.

Don't let today's stress rob me of tomorrow's peace.

I am willing to fail in order to succeed.

Every day, I am regaining my energy & control over my life.

"Adopting the right attitude can convert a negative stress into a positive one." Hans Selye

When we focus less on our problems, we open our minds to new possibilities.

Adequate sleep helps me deal better with daily stresses.

"It's not what happens to you, but how you react to it that matters." - Epictetus

It is alright to set limits with others in order to take care of my own health.

"The only difference between a good day and a bad day is my attitude." – Dennis S. Brown

I allow peace & harmony to surround me at all times.

Date: _____ Wake-Up Time Today: _____ Hours of Sleep I Got Last Night: _____

My Mood: Morning   Afternoon   Evening

Food/Beverages I Had Today:

B _____

L _____

D _____

Snacks _____

_____

What I Did for Exercise Today: **My Water Intake:**

_____

_____

_____

Did I feel any of the following today?:

- ☐ Sadness and/or crying
- ☐ Hopeless
- ☐ No energy/fatigue/lethargy
- ☐ Difficulty concentrating/making decisions
- ☐ Appetite is increased or decreased
- ☐ Lack of motivation
- ☐ Anger/frustration
- ☐ Lack of interest in activities I normally enjoy

What caused me to feel negative emotions today?

_____

_____

_____

Go to your doctor/medical professional immediately if you are suicidal or your mood is not getting better.

Is there anything that I could have done to improve my day?

_____

_____

_____

_____

Positive things that happened today:

_____

_____

_____

_____

Today, I am grateful for:

_____

_____

_____

_____

Goals/things I can do to make tomorrow better:

_____

_____

_____

_____

Positive Affirmation:

_____

_____

_____

One day at a time

Date: _____   Wake-Up Time Today: _____   Hours of Sleep I Got Last Night: _____

My Mood: Morning   Afternoon   Evening

Food/Beverages I Had Today: **What I Did for Exercise Today:**   **My Water Intake:**

B _____   _____

L _____   _____

D _____   _____

Snacks _____   _____

_____

Did I feel any of the following today?:   **What caused me to feel negative emotions today?**

- ☐ Sadness and/or crying   _____
- ☐ Hopeless   _____
- ☐ No energy/fatigue/lethargy   _____
- ☐ Difficulty concentrating/making decisions   _____
- ☐ Appetite is increased or decreased
- ☐ Lack of motivation   ****Go to your doctor/medical professional
- ☐ Anger/frustration   immediately if you are suicidal or your mood is not
- ☐ Lack of interest in activities I normally enjoy   getting better.****

Is there anything that I could have done to improve my day?   **Positive things that happened today:**

_____   _____

_____   _____

_____   _____

_____   _____

Today, I am grateful for: **Goals/things I can do to make tomorrow better:**

_____   _____

_____   _____

_____   _____

Positive Affirmation:

_____

_____

_____

LIFE IS TOUGH ★★★ BUT ★★★ so ARE YOU

Date: _____ Wake-Up Time Today: _____ Hours of Sleep I Got Last Night: _____

My Mood: Morning   Afternoon   Evening

What I Did for Exercise Today: **My Water Intake:**

B _____
    Food/Beverages I Had Today:
L _____
D _____
Snacks _____
    _____

Did I feel any of the following today?:

- ☐ Sadness and/or crying
- ☐ Hopeless
- ☐ No energy/fatigue/lethargy
- ☐ Difficulty concentrating/making decisions
- ☐ Appetite is increased or decreased
- ☐ Lack of motivation
- ☐ Anger/frustration
- ☐ Lack of interest in activities I normally enjoy

What caused me to feel negative emotions today?

_____
_____
_____
_____

Go to your doctor/medical professional immediately if you are suicidal or your mood is not getting better.

Is there anything that I could have done to improve my day?

_____
_____
_____
_____
_____

Positive things that happened today:

_____
_____
_____
_____
_____

Today, I am grateful for:

_____
_____
_____
_____

Goals/things I can do to make tomorrow better:

_____
_____
_____
_____

Positive Affirmation:

_____
_____
_____

you GOT this

Date: _____ Wake-Up Time Today: _____ Hours of Sleep I Got Last Night: _____

My Mood: Morning   Afternoon   Evening

Food/Beverages I Had Today:

B   _____

L   _____

D   _____

Snacks _____

_____

What I Did for Exercise Today: **My Water Intake:**

_____

_____

_____

_____

Did I feel any of the following today?:

- ☐ Sadness and/or crying
- ☐ Hopeless
- ☐ No energy/fatigue/lethargy
- ☐ Difficulty concentrating/making decisions
- ☐ Appetite is increased or decreased
- ☐ Lack of motivation
- ☐ Anger/frustration
- ☐ Lack of interest in activities I normally enjoy

What caused me to feel negative emotions today?

_____

_____

_____

Go to your doctor/medical professional immediately if you are suicidal or your mood is not getting better.

Is there anything that I could have done to improve my day?

_____

_____

_____

_____

_____

Positive things that happened today:

_____

_____

_____

_____

_____

Today, I am grateful for:

_____

_____

_____

Goals/things I can do to make tomorrow better:

_____

_____

_____

Positive Affirmation:

_____

_____

_____

Choose joy

Date: _____ Wake-Up Time Today: _____ Hours of Sleep I Got Last Night: _____

My Mood: Morning   Afternoon   Evening

Food/Beverages I Had Today: **What I Did for Exercise Today:**   **My Water Intake:**

B _____   _____

L _____   _____

D _____   _____

Snacks _____   _____

_____

Did I feel any of the following today?:   **What caused me to feel negative emotions today?**

- ☐ Sadness and/or crying   _____
- ☐ Hopeless
- ☐ No energy/fatigue/lethargy   _____
- ☐ Difficulty concentrating/making decisions
- ☐ Appetite is increased or decreased   _____
- ☐ Lack of motivation
- ☐ Anger/frustration   _____
- ☐ Lack of interest in activities I normally enjoy

**Go to your doctor/medical professional
immediately if you are suicidal or your mood is not
getting better.**

**Is there anything that I could have done to
improve my day?**   **Positive things that happened today:**

_____   _____

_____   _____

_____   _____

_____   _____

_____   _____

Today, I am grateful for: **Goals/things I can do to make tomorrow better:**

_____   _____

_____   _____

_____   _____

_____   _____

Positive Affirmation:

_____

_____   Every
                                                                              DAY
                                                                              IS A
                                                                              NEW
                                                                              beginning

Date: _____ Wake-Up Time Today: _____ Hours of Sleep I Got Last Night: _____

My Mood: Morning Afternoon Evening

Food/Beverages I Had Today:

B _____

L _____

D _____

Snacks _____

_____

Did I feel any of the following today?:

- ☐ Sadness and/or crying
- ☐ Hopeless
- ☐ No energy/fatigue/lethargy
- ☐ Difficulty concentrating/making decisions
- ☐ Appetite is increased or decreased
- ☐ Lack of motivation
- ☐ Anger/frustration
- ☐ Lack of interest in activities I normally enjoy

Is there anything that I could have done to improve my day?

_____

_____

_____

_____

_____

Today, I am grateful for:

_____

_____

_____

_____

Positive Affirmation: _____

_____

_____

What I Did for Exercise Today: **My Water Intake:**

_____

_____

_____

_____

What caused me to feel negative emotions today?

_____

_____

_____

Go to your doctor/medical professional immediately if you are suicidal or your mood is not getting better.

Positive things that happened today:

_____

_____

_____

_____

_____

Goals/things I can do to make tomorrow better:

_____

_____

_____

_____

A DAY WITHOUT
laughter
IS A DAY WASTED

Date: _____ Wake-Up Time Today: _____ Hours of Sleep I Got Last Night: _____

My Mood: Morning   Afternoon   Evening

Food/Beverages I Had Today:

B _____

L _____

D _____

Snacks _____

_____

What I Did for Exercise Today: **My Water Intake:**

_____

_____

_____

Did I feel any of the following today?:

- ☐ Sadness and/or crying
- ☐ Hopeless
- ☐ No energy/fatigue/lethargy
- ☐ Difficulty concentrating/making decisions
- ☐ Appetite is increased or decreased
- ☐ Lack of motivation
- ☐ Anger/frustration
- ☐ Lack of interest in activities I normally enjoy

What caused me to feel negative emotions today?

_____

_____

_____

Go to your doctor/medical professional immediately if you are suicidal or your mood is not getting better.

Is there anything that I could have done to improve my day?

_____

_____

_____

_____

Positive things that happened today:

_____

_____

_____

_____

Today, I am grateful for:

_____

_____

_____

Goals/things I can do to make tomorrow better:

_____

_____

_____

Positive Affirmation: _____

_____

_____

The greater the ✦ **STORM** ✦ *the brighter the* **RAINBOW**

More of My Thoughts

My Favorite Positive Affirmations

This is the place to record your favorite affirmations that you can refer to anytime you feel like you need a boost in your mind, body, or spirit.

POSITIVE mind
POSITIVE vibes
POSITIVE life

Date: _____ Wake-Up Time Today: _____ Hours of Sleep I Got Last Night: _____

My Mood: Morning   Afternoon   Evening

Food/Beverages I Had Today: **What I Did for Exercise Today:**   **My Water Intake:**

B _____   _____

L _____   _____

D _____   _____

Snacks _____   _____

_____

Did I feel any of the following today?:   **What caused me to feel negative emotions today?**

☐ Sadness and/or crying   _____
☐ Hopeless
☐ No energy/fatigue/lethargy   _____
☐ Difficulty concentrating/making decisions
☐ Appetite is increased or decreased   _____
☐ Lack of motivation
☐ Anger/frustration   ****Go to your doctor/medical professional
☐ Lack of interest in activities I normally enjoy   immediately if you are suicidal or your mood is not
                                        getting better.****

Is there anything that I could have done to improve my day?   **Positive things that happened today:**

_____   _____

_____   _____

_____   _____

_____   _____

Today, I am grateful for: **Goals/things I can do to make tomorrow better:**

_____   _____

_____   _____

_____   _____

Positive Affirmation: _____

_____

_____

One day at a time

Date: _____ Wake-Up Time Today: _____ Hours of Sleep I Got Last Night: _____

My Mood: Morning   Afternoon   Evening

Food/Beverages I Had Today:

B _____

L _____

D _____

Snacks _____

_____

What I Did for Exercise Today: **My Water Intake:**

_____

_____

_____

Did I feel any of the following today?:

- ☐ Sadness and/or crying
- ☐ Hopeless
- ☐ No energy/fatigue/lethargy
- ☐ Difficulty concentrating/making decisions
- ☐ Appetite is increased or decreased
- ☐ Lack of motivation
- ☐ Anger/frustration
- ☐ Lack of interest in activities I normally enjoy

What caused me to feel negative emotions today?

_____

_____

_____

_____

Go to your doctor/medical professional immediately if you are suicidal or your mood is not getting better.

Is there anything that I could have done to improve my day?

_____

_____

_____

_____

Positive things that happened today:

_____

_____

_____

_____

Today, I am grateful for:

_____

_____

_____

Goals/things I can do to make tomorrow better:

_____

_____

_____

Positive Affirmation:

_____

_____

LIFE IS TOUGH
BUT
so
ARE YOU

Date: _____   Wake-Up Time Today: _____   Hours of Sleep I Got Last Night: _____

My Mood: Morning   Afternoon   Evening

What I Did for Exercise Today: **My Water Intake:**

B _____
                    Food/Beverages I Had Today:
L _____

D _____

Snacks _____

_____

Did I feel any of the following today?:

- ☐ Sadness and/or crying
- ☐ Hopeless
- ☐ No energy/fatigue/lethargy
- ☐ Difficulty concentrating/making decisions
- ☐ Appetite is increased or decreased
- ☐ Lack of motivation
- ☐ Anger/frustration
- ☐ Lack of interest in activities I normally enjoy

What caused me to feel negative emotions today?

_____

_____

_____

Go to your doctor/medical professional immediately if you are suicidal or your mood is not getting better.

Is there anything that I could have done to improve my day?

_____

_____

_____

_____

Positive things that happened today:

_____

_____

_____

_____

Today, I am grateful for:

_____

_____

_____

Goals/things I can do to make tomorrow better:

_____

_____

_____

Positive Affirmation:

_____

_____

_____

you GOT this

Date: _____ Wake-Up Time Today: _____ Hours of Sleep I Got Last Night: _____

My Mood: Morning   Afternoon   Evening

Food/Beverages I Had Today: **What I Did for Exercise Today:**   **My Water Intake:**

B _____   _____

L _____   _____

D _____   _____

Snacks _____   _____

_____

Did I feel any of the following today?:

- ☐ Sadness and/or crying
- ☐ Hopeless
- ☐ No energy/fatigue/lethargy
- ☐ Difficulty concentrating/making decisions
- ☐ Appetite is increased or decreased
- ☐ Lack of motivation
- ☐ Anger/frustration
- ☐ Lack of interest in activities I normally enjoy

What caused me to feel negative emotions today?

_____

_____

_____

Go to your doctor/medical professional immediately if you are suicidal or your mood is not getting better.

Is there anything that I could have done to improve my day?

_____
_____
_____
_____
_____

Positive things that happened today:

_____
_____
_____
_____
_____

Today, I am grateful for:

_____
_____
_____
_____

Goals/things I can do to make tomorrow better:

_____
_____
_____
_____

Positive Affirmation:

_____
_____
_____

Choose joy

Date: _____   Wake-Up Time Today: _____   Hours of Sleep I Got Last Night: _____

My Mood: Morning   Afternoon   Evening

Food/Beverages I Had Today:

B _____

L _____

D _____

Snacks _____

_____

What I Did for Exercise Today: **My Water Intake:**

_____

_____

_____

_____

Did I feel any of the following today?:

- ☐ Sadness and/or crying
- ☐ Hopeless
- ☐ No energy/fatigue/lethargy
- ☐ Difficulty concentrating/making decisions
- ☐ Appetite is increased or decreased
- ☐ Lack of motivation
- ☐ Anger/frustration
- ☐ Lack of interest in activities I normally enjoy

What caused me to feel negative emotions today?

_____

_____

_____

_____

Go to your doctor/medical professional immediately if you are suicidal or your mood is not getting better.

Is there anything that I could have done to improve my day?

_____

_____

_____

_____

_____

Positive things that happened today:

_____

_____

_____

_____

_____

Today, I am grateful for:

_____

_____

_____

_____

Goals/things I can do to make tomorrow better:

_____

_____

_____

_____

Positive Affirmation:

_____

_____

_____

Date: _____ Wake-Up Time Today: _____ Hours of Sleep I Got Last Night: _____

My Mood: Morning   Afternoon   Evening

Food/Beverages I Had Today: **What I Did for Exercise Today:**   **My Water Intake:**

B _____   _____

L _____   _____

D _____   _____

Snacks _____   _____

_____

Did I feel any of the following today?:

- ☐ Sadness and/or crying
- ☐ Hopeless
- ☐ No energy/fatigue/lethargy
- ☐ Difficulty concentrating/making decisions
- ☐ Appetite is increased or decreased
- ☐ Lack of motivation
- ☐ Anger/frustration
- ☐ Lack of interest in activities I normally enjoy

What caused me to feel negative emotions today?

_____
_____
_____

Go to your doctor/medical professional immediately if you are suicidal or your mood is not getting better.

Is there anything that I could have done to improve my day?

_____
_____
_____
_____
_____

Positive things that happened today:

_____
_____
_____
_____
_____

Today, I am grateful for:

_____
_____
_____
_____

Goals/things I can do to make tomorrow better:

_____
_____
_____
_____

Positive Affirmation:

_____
_____
_____

A DAY WITHOUT laughter IS A DAY WASTED

Date: _____ Wake-Up Time Today: _____ Hours of Sleep I Got Last Night: _____

My Mood: Morning   Afternoon   Evening

Food/Beverages I Had Today: **What I Did for Exercise Today:**   **My Water Intake:**

B _____   _____

L _____   _____

D _____   _____

Snacks _____   _____

_____

Did I feel any of the following today?:   **What caused me to feel negative emotions today?**

- ☐ Sadness and/or crying
- ☐ Hopeless
- ☐ No energy/fatigue/lethargy
- ☐ Difficulty concentrating/making decisions
- ☐ Appetite is increased or decreased
- ☐ Lack of motivation
- ☐ Anger/frustration
- ☐ Lack of interest in activities I normally enjoy

_____

_____

_____

Go to your doctor/medical professional immediately if you are suicidal or your mood is not getting better.

Is there anything that I could have done to improve my day?   **Positive things that happened today:**

_____   _____

_____   _____

_____   _____

_____   _____

_____   _____

Today, I am grateful for: **Goals/things I can do to make tomorrow better:**

_____   _____

_____   _____

_____   _____

_____   _____

Positive Affirmation:

_____

_____   *The greater the*
                                        ★ STORM ★
_____   *the brighter the*
                                        RAINBOW

More of My Thoughts

My Favorite Positive Affirmations

Great things *never came from* **comfort** ZONES

Date: _____ Wake-Up Time Today: _____ Hours of Sleep I Got Last Night: _____

My Mood: Morning   Afternoon   Evening

Food/Beverages I Had Today: **What I Did for Exercise Today:**   **My Water Intake:**

B _____   _____

L _____   _____

D _____   _____

Snacks _____   _____

_____

Did I feel any of the following today?:   **What caused me to feel negative emotions today?**

- ☐ Sadness and/or crying   _____
- ☐ Hopeless   _____
- ☐ No energy/fatigue/lethargy   _____
- ☐ Difficulty concentrating/making decisions _____
- ☐ Appetite is increased or decreased
- ☐ Lack of motivation   ****Go to your doctor/medical professional
- ☐ Anger/frustration   immediately if you are suicidal or your mood is not
- ☐ Lack of interest in activities I normally enjoy   getting better.****

Is there anything that I could have done to   **Positive things that happened today:
improve my day?**

_____   _____

_____   _____

_____   _____

_____   _____

_____   _____

Today, I am grateful for: **Goals/things I can do to make tomorrow better:**

_____   _____

_____   _____

_____   _____

_____   _____

Positive Affirmation: _____

_____

_____   *One day at a time*

Date: _____   Wake-Up Time Today: _____   Hours of Sleep I Got Last Night: _____

My Mood: Morning   Afternoon   Evening

Food/Beverages I Had Today: **What I Did for Exercise Today:**   **My Water Intake:**

B _____   _____

L _____   _____

D _____   _____

Snacks _____   _____

_____

Did I feel any of the following today?:

- ☐ Sadness and/or crying
- ☐ Hopeless
- ☐ No energy/fatigue/lethargy
- ☐ Difficulty concentrating/making decisions
- ☐ Appetite is increased or decreased
- ☐ Lack of motivation
- ☐ Anger/frustration
- ☐ Lack of interest in activities I normally enjoy

What caused me to feel negative emotions today?

_____

_____

_____

Go to your doctor/medical professional immediately if you are suicidal or your mood is not getting better.

Is there anything that I could have done to improve my day?

_____

_____

_____

_____

_____

Positive things that happened today:

_____

_____

_____

_____

_____

Today, I am grateful for:

_____

_____

_____

_____

Goals/things I can do to make tomorrow better:

_____

_____

_____

_____

Positive Affirmation:

_____

_____

LIFE IS TOUGH
★★★ BUT ★★★
SO
ARE YOU

Date: _____ Wake-Up Time Today: _____ Hours of Sleep I Got Last Night: _____

My Mood: Morning   Afternoon   Evening

What I Did for Exercise Today: **My Water Intake:**

B _____
Food/Beverages I Had Today:
L _____
D _____
Snacks _____
_____

Did I feel any of the following today?:

- ☐ Sadness and/or crying
- ☐ Hopeless
- ☐ No energy/fatigue/lethargy
- ☐ Difficulty concentrating/making decisions
- ☐ Appetite is increased or decreased
- ☐ Lack of motivation
- ☐ Anger/frustration
- ☐ Lack of interest in activities I normally enjoy

What caused me to feel negative emotions today?

_____
_____
_____

Go to your doctor/medical professional immediately if you are suicidal or your mood is not getting better.

Is there anything that I could have done to improve my day?

_____
_____
_____
_____
_____

Positive things that happened today:

_____
_____
_____
_____
_____

Today, I am grateful for:

_____
_____
_____
_____

Goals/things I can do to make tomorrow better:

_____
_____
_____
_____

Positive Affirmation:

_____
_____
_____

you GOT this

Date: _____   Wake-Up Time Today: _____   Hours of Sleep I Got Last Night: _____

My Mood: Morning   Afternoon   Evening

Food/Beverages I Had Today: What I Did for Exercise Today: **My Water Intake:**

B _____   _____

L _____   _____

D _____   _____

Snacks _____   _____

_____   _____

Did I feel any of the following today?:   **What caused me to feel negative emotions today?**

- ☐ Sadness and/or crying   _____
- ☐ Hopeless
- ☐ No energy/fatigue/lethargy   _____
- ☐ Difficulty concentrating/making decisions
- ☐ Appetite is increased or decreased   _____
- ☐ Lack of motivation
- ☐ Anger/frustration   ****Go to your doctor/medical professional
- ☐ Lack of interest in activities I normally enjoy   immediately if you are suicidal or your mood is not
                                         getting better.****

Is there anything that I could have done to   **Positive things that happened today:
improve my day?**

_____   _____

_____   _____

_____   _____

_____   _____

_____   _____

Today, I am grateful for: **Goals/things I can do to make tomorrow better:**

_____   _____

_____   _____

_____   _____

_____   _____

Positive Affirmation: _____

_____   *Choose joy*

_____

Date: _____ Wake-Up Time Today: _____ Hours of Sleep I Got Last Night: _____

My Mood: Morning   Afternoon   Evening

Food/Beverages I Had Today: **What I Did for Exercise Today:**   **My Water Intake:**

B _____   _____

L _____   _____

D _____   _____

Snacks _____   _____

_____

Did I feel any of the following today?:   **What caused me to feel negative emotions today?**

- ☐ Sadness and/or crying   _____
- ☐ Hopeless   _____
- ☐ No energy/fatigue/lethargy   _____
- ☐ Difficulty concentrating/making decisions
- ☐ Appetite is increased or decreased
- ☐ Lack of motivation   ****Go to your doctor/medical professional
- ☐ Anger/frustration   immediately if you are suicidal or your mood is not
- ☐ Lack of interest in activities I normally enjoy getting better.****

Is there anything that I could have done to   **Positive things that happened today:
improve my day?**

_____   _____

_____   _____

_____   _____

_____   _____

Today, I am grateful for: **Goals/things I can do to make tomorrow better:**

_____   _____

_____   _____

_____   _____

Positive Affirmation:

_____

_____   Every DAY IS A NEW beginning

_____

Date: _____   Wake-Up Time Today: _____   Hours of Sleep I Got Last Night: _____

My Mood: Morning   Afternoon   Evening

Food/Beverages I Had Today: **What I Did for Exercise Today:**   **My Water Intake:**

B _____   _____

L _____   _____

D _____   _____

Snacks _____   _____

_____

Did I feel any of the following today?:   **What caused me to feel negative emotions today?**

- ☐ Sadness and/or crying
- ☐ Hopeless
- ☐ No energy/fatigue/lethargy
- ☐ Difficulty concentrating/making decisions
- ☐ Appetite is increased or decreased
- ☐ Lack of motivation
- ☐ Anger/frustration
- ☐ Lack of interest in activities I normally enjoy

Go to your doctor/medical professional immediately if you are suicidal or your mood is not getting better.

Is there anything that I could have done to improve my day?   **Positive things that happened today:**

Today, I am grateful for: **Goals/things I can do to make tomorrow better:**

Positive Affirmation: _____

A DAY WITHOUT *laughter* IS A DAY WASTED

Date: _____   Wake-Up Time Today: _____   Hours of Sleep I Got Last Night: _____

My Mood: Morning   Afternoon   Evening

Food/Beverages I Had Today: **What I Did for Exercise Today:**   **My Water Intake:**

B   _____   _____

L   _____   _____

D   _____   _____

Snacks _____   _____

_____

Did I feel any of the following today?:   **What caused me to feel negative emotions today?**

- ☐ Sadness and/or crying
- ☐ Hopeless
- ☐ No energy/fatigue/lethargy
- ☐ Difficulty concentrating/making decisions
- ☐ Appetite is increased or decreased
- ☐ Lack of motivation
- ☐ Anger/frustration
- ☐ Lack of interest in activities I normally enjoy

_____

_____

_____

Go to your doctor/medical professional immediately if you are suicidal or your mood is not getting better.

Is there anything that I could have done to improve my day?   **Positive things that happened today:**

_____   _____

_____   _____

_____   _____

_____   _____

_____   _____

Today, I am grateful for: **Goals/things I can do to make tomorrow better:**

_____   _____

_____   _____

_____   _____

_____   _____

Positive Affirmation:

_____

_____   *The greater the*
✦ STORM ✦
the brighter the
RAINBOW

_____

More of My Thoughts

My Favorite Positive Affirmations

I AM WORKING
on
myself
FOR
myself

I'M AMAZING

Date: _____   Wake-Up Time Today: _____   Hours of Sleep I Got Last Night: _____

My Mood: Morning   Afternoon   Evening

Food/Beverages I Had Today: **What I Did for Exercise Today:**   **My Water Intake:**

B _____   _____

L _____   _____

D _____   _____

Snacks _____   _____

_____

Did I feel any of the following today?:   **What caused me to feel negative emotions today?**

- ☐ Sadness and/or crying   _____
- ☐ Hopeless
- ☐ No energy/fatigue/lethargy   _____
- ☐ Difficulty concentrating/making decisions
- ☐ Appetite is increased or decreased   _____
- ☐ Lack of motivation
- ☐ Anger/frustration   **Go to your doctor/medical professional
- ☐ Lack of interest in activities I normally enjoy   immediately if you are suicidal or your mood is not
                                             getting better.**

Is there anything that I could have done to   **Positive things that happened today:**
improve my day?

_____   _____

_____   _____

_____   _____

_____   _____

_____   _____

Today, I am grateful for: **Goals/things I can do to make tomorrow better:**

_____   _____

_____   _____

_____   _____

_____   _____

Positive Affirmation: _____

_____

_____   One day at a time

Date: _____ Wake-Up Time Today: _____ Hours of Sleep I Got Last Night: _____

My Mood: Morning   Afternoon   Evening

Food/Beverages I Had Today: **What I Did for Exercise Today:**   **My Water Intake:**

B _____   _____

L _____   _____

D _____   _____

Snacks _____   _____

_____

Did I feel any of the following today?:   **What caused me to feel negative emotions today?**

- ☐ Sadness and/or crying   _____
- ☐ Hopeless   _____
- ☐ No energy/fatigue/lethargy   _____
- ☐ Difficulty concentrating/making decisions   _____
- ☐ Appetite is increased or decreased
- ☐ Lack of motivation   ****Go to your doctor/medical professional
- ☐ Anger/frustration   immediately if you are suicidal or your mood is not
- ☐ Lack of interest in activities I normally enjoy   getting better.****

Is there anything that I could have done to improve my day?   **Positive things that happened today:**

_____   _____

_____   _____

_____   _____

_____   _____

_____   _____

Today, I am grateful for: **Goals/things I can do to make tomorrow better:**

_____   _____

_____   _____

_____   _____

_____   _____

Positive Affirmation:

_____

_____   LIFE IS TOUGH
                                         ★ ★ ★ BUT ★ ★ ★
_____   SO
                                         ARE YOU

Date: _____ Wake-Up Time Today: _____ Hours of Sleep I Got Last Night: _____

My Mood: Morning   Afternoon   Evening

What I Did for Exercise Today: **My Water Intake:**

B _____

Food/Beverages I Had Today:

L _____

D _____

Snacks _____

_____

_____

_____

_____

_____

Did I feel any of the following today?:

- ☐ Sadness and/or crying
- ☐ Hopeless
- ☐ No energy/fatigue/lethargy
- ☐ Difficulty concentrating/making decisions
- ☐ Appetite is increased or decreased
- ☐ Lack of motivation
- ☐ Anger/frustration
- ☐ Lack of interest in activities I normally enjoy

What caused me to feel negative emotions today?

_____

_____

_____

Go to your doctor/medical professional immediately if you are suicidal or your mood is not getting better.

Is there anything that I could have done to improve my day?

_____

_____

_____

_____

_____

Positive things that happened today:

_____

_____

_____

_____

_____

Today, I am grateful for:

_____

_____

_____

_____

Goals/things I can do to make tomorrow better:

_____

_____

_____

_____

Positive Affirmation:

_____

_____

_____

you GOT this

Date: _____   Wake-Up Time Today: _____   Hours of Sleep I Got Last Night: _____

My Mood: Morning   Afternoon   Evening

Food/Beverages I Had Today: **What I Did for Exercise Today:**   **My Water Intake:**

B _____   _____

L _____   _____

D _____   _____

Snacks _____   _____

_____

Did I feel any of the following today?:

- ☐ Sadness and/or crying
- ☐ Hopeless
- ☐ No energy/fatigue/lethargy
- ☐ Difficulty concentrating/making decisions
- ☐ Appetite is increased or decreased
- ☐ Lack of motivation
- ☐ Anger/frustration
- ☐ Lack of interest in activities I normally enjoy

What caused me to feel negative emotions today?

_____

_____

_____

_____

Go to your doctor/medical professional immediately if you are suicidal or your mood is not getting better.

Is there anything that I could have done to improve my day?

_____

_____

_____

_____

_____

Positive things that happened today:

_____

_____

_____

_____

Today, I am grateful for:

_____

_____

_____

_____

Goals/things I can do to make tomorrow better:

_____

_____

_____

_____

Positive Affirmation:

_____

_____

_____

Choose joy

Date: _____ Wake-Up Time Today: _____ Hours of Sleep I Got Last Night: _____

My Mood: Morning   Afternoon   Evening

Food/Beverages I Had Today: **What I Did for Exercise Today:**   **My Water Intake:**

B _____   _____

L _____   _____

D _____   _____

Snacks _____   _____

_____

Did I feel any of the following today?:   **What caused me to feel negative emotions today?**

- ☐ Sadness and/or crying   _____
- ☐ Hopeless
- ☐ No energy/fatigue/lethargy   _____
- ☐ Difficulty concentrating/making decisions
- ☐ Appetite is increased or decreased   _____
- ☐ Lack of motivation
- ☐ Anger/frustration   **Go to your doctor/medical professional
- ☐ Lack of interest in activities I normally enjoy   immediately if you are suicidal or your mood is not
                                             getting better.****

Is there anything that I could have done to   **Positive things that happened today:
improve my day?**

_____   _____

_____   _____

_____   _____

_____   _____

_____   _____

Today, I am grateful for: **Goals/things I can do to make tomorrow better:**

_____   _____

_____   _____

_____   _____

Positive Affirmation:

_____

_____

Every DAY IS A NEW beginning

Date: _____   Wake-Up Time Today: _____   Hours of Sleep I Got Last Night: _____

My Mood: Morning   Afternoon   Evening

Food/Beverages I Had Today: **What I Did for Exercise Today:**   **My Water Intake:**

B   _____   _____

L   _____   _____

D   _____   _____

Snacks _____   _____

_____

Did I feel any of the following today?:   **What caused me to feel negative emotions today?**

☐   Sadness and/or crying   _____
☐   Hopeless   _____
☐   No energy/fatigue/lethargy   _____
☐   Difficulty concentrating/making decisions
☐   Appetite is increased or decreased   _____
☐   Lack of motivation
☐   Anger/frustration   **Go to your doctor/medical professional
☐   Lack of interest in activities I normally enjoy   immediately if you are suicidal or your mood is not getting better.**

Is there anything that I could have done to improve my day?   **Positive things that happened today:**

_____   _____

_____   _____

_____   _____

_____   _____

_____   _____

Today, I am grateful for: **Goals/things I can do to make tomorrow better:**

_____   _____

_____   _____

_____   _____

Positive Affirmation: _____

_____

_____

A DAY WITHOUT *laughter* IS A DAY WASTED

Date: _____   Wake-Up Time Today: _____   Hours of Sleep I Got Last Night: _____

My Mood: Morning   Afternoon   Evening

Food/Beverages I Had Today: **What I Did for Exercise Today:**   **My Water Intake:**

B _____   _____

L _____   _____

D _____   _____

Snacks _____   _____

_____

Did I feel any of the following today?:   **What caused me to feel negative emotions today?**

☐ Sadness and/or crying   _____
☐ Hopeless
☐ No energy/fatigue/lethargy   _____
☐ Difficulty concentrating/making decisions
☐ Appetite is increased or decreased   _____
☐ Lack of motivation
☐ Anger/frustration   ****Go to your doctor/medical professional
☐ Lack of interest in activities I normally enjoy immediately if you are suicidal or your mood is not
                                                    getting better.****

Is there anything that I could have done to   **Positive things that happened today:**
improve my day?

_____   _____

_____   _____

_____   _____

_____   _____

Today, I am grateful for: **Goals/things I can do to make tomorrow better:**

_____   _____

_____   _____

_____   _____

Positive Affirmation: _____

_____

The greater the
✦ STORM ✦
the brighter the
RAINBOW

More of My Thoughts

My Positive Affirmations

A DAY WITHOUT

laughter

IS A DAY WASTED

Date: _____ Wake-Up Time Today: _____ Hours of Sleep I Got Last Night: _____

My Mood: Morning   Afternoon   Evening

Food/Beverages I Had Today: **What I Did for Exercise Today:**   **My Water Intake:**

B _____   _____

L _____   _____

D _____   _____

Snacks _____   _____

_____   _____

Did I feel any of the following today?:   **What caused me to feel negative emotions today?**

- [ ] Sadness and/or crying
- [ ] Hopeless
- [ ] No energy/fatigue/lethargy
- [ ] Difficulty concentrating/making decisions
- [ ] Appetite is increased or decreased
- [ ] Lack of motivation
- [ ] Anger/frustration
- [ ] Lack of interest in activities I normally enjoy

Go to your doctor/medical professional immediately if you are suicidal or your mood is not getting better.

Is there anything that I could have done to improve my day?

Positive things that happened today:

Today, I am grateful for:

Goals/things I can do to make tomorrow better:

Positive Affirmation:

One day at a time

Date: _____   Wake-Up Time Today: _____   Hours of Sleep I Got Last Night: _____

My Mood: Morning   Afternoon   Evening

Food/Beverages I Had Today: **What I Did for Exercise Today:**   **My Water Intake:**

B _____   _____

L _____   _____

D _____   _____

Snacks _____   _____

_____

Did I feel any of the following today?:   **What caused me to feel negative emotions today?**

- [ ] Sadness and/or crying   _____
- [ ] Hopeless
- [ ] No energy/fatigue/lethargy   _____
- [ ] Difficulty concentrating/making decisions
- [ ] Appetite is increased or decreased   _____
- [ ] Lack of motivation
- [ ] Anger/frustration   ****Go to your doctor/medical professional
- [ ] Lack of interest in activities I normally enjoy   immediately if you are suicidal or your mood is not
                                           getting better.****

Is there anything that I could have done to improve my day?   **Positive things that happened today:**

_____   _____

_____   _____

_____   _____

_____   _____

_____   _____

Today, I am grateful for: **Goals/things I can do to make tomorrow better:**

_____   _____

_____   _____

_____   _____

Positive Affirmation: _____

_____

_____

LIFE IS TOUGH ★★★ BUT ★★★ *so* **ARE YOU**

Date: _____   Wake-Up Time Today: _____   Hours of Sleep I Got Last Night: _____

My Mood: Morning   Afternoon   Evening

What I Did for Exercise Today: My Water Intake:

B _____
Food/Beverages I Had Today:
L _____

D _____

Snacks _____

_____

Did I feel any of the following today?:

- ☐ Sadness and/or crying
- ☐ Hopeless
- ☐ No energy/fatigue/lethargy
- ☐ Difficulty concentrating/making decisions
- ☐ Appetite is increased or decreased
- ☐ Lack of motivation
- ☐ Anger/frustration
- ☐ Lack of interest in activities I normally enjoy

What caused me to feel negative emotions today?

_____

_____

_____

_____

Go to your doctor/medical professional immediately if you are suicidal or your mood is not getting better.

Is there anything that I could have done to improve my day?

_____

_____

_____

_____

_____

Positive things that happened today:

_____

_____

_____

_____

_____

Today, I am grateful for:

_____

_____

_____

_____

Goals/things I can do to make tomorrow better:

_____

_____

_____

_____

Positive Affirmation: _____

_____

_____

you GOT this

Date: _____   Wake-Up Time Today: _____   Hours of Sleep I Got Last Night: _____

My Mood: Morning   Afternoon   Evening

Food/Beverages I Had Today: **What I Did for Exercise Today:**   **My Water Intake:**

B _____   _____

L _____   _____

D _____   _____

Snacks _____   _____

Did I feel any of the following today?:   **What caused me to feel negative emotions today?**

☐ Sadness and/or crying
☐ Hopeless   _____
☐ No energy/fatigue/lethargy
☐ Difficulty concentrating/making decisions   _____
☐ Appetite is increased or decreased
☐ Lack of motivation   _____
☐ Anger/frustration
☐ Lack of interest in activities I normally enjoy

Go to your doctor/medical professional immediately if you are suicidal or your mood is not getting better.

Is there anything that I could have done to improve my day?   **Positive things that happened today:**

_____   _____
_____   _____
_____   _____
_____   _____
_____   _____

Today, I am grateful for: **Goals/things I can do to make tomorrow better:**

_____   _____
_____   _____
_____   _____

Positive Affirmation:
_____
_____   *Choose joy*
_____

Date: _____ Wake-Up Time Today: _____ Hours of Sleep I Got Last Night: _____

My Mood: Morning   Afternoon   Evening

Food/Beverages I Had Today:

B _____

L _____

D _____

Snacks _____

_____

What I Did for Exercise Today: **My Water Intake:**

_____

_____

_____

_____

Did I feel any of the following today?:

☐ Sadness and/or crying
☐ Hopeless
☐ No energy/fatigue/lethargy
☐ Difficulty concentrating/making decisions
☐ Appetite is increased or decreased
☐ Lack of motivation
☐ Anger/frustration
☐ Lack of interest in activities I normally enjoy

What caused me to feel negative emotions today?

_____

_____

_____

_____

Go to your doctor/medical professional immediately if you are suicidal or your mood is not getting better.

Is there anything that I could have done to improve my day?

_____
_____
_____
_____
_____

Positive things that happened today:

_____
_____
_____
_____
_____

Today, I am grateful for:

_____
_____
_____
_____

Goals/things I can do to make tomorrow better:

_____
_____
_____
_____

Positive Affirmation:

_____
_____
_____

Every DAY IS A NEW beginning

Date: _____ Wake-Up Time Today: _____ Hours of Sleep I Got Last Night: _____

My Mood: Morning   Afternoon   Evening

Food/Beverages I Had Today:

B _____

L _____

D _____

Snacks _____

_____

What I Did for Exercise Today: **My Water Intake:**

_____

_____

_____

Did I feel any of the following today?:

- ☐ Sadness and/or crying
- ☐ Hopeless
- ☐ No energy/fatigue/lethargy
- ☐ Difficulty concentrating/making decisions
- ☐ Appetite is increased or decreased
- ☐ Lack of motivation
- ☐ Anger/frustration
- ☐ Lack of interest in activities I normally enjoy

What caused me to feel negative emotions today?

_____

_____

_____

Go to your doctor/medical professional immediately if you are suicidal or your mood is not getting better.

Is there anything that I could have done to improve my day?

_____

_____

_____

_____

_____

Positive things that happened today:

_____

_____

_____

_____

_____

Today, I am grateful for:

_____

_____

_____

Goals/things I can do to make tomorrow better:

_____

_____

_____

Positive Affirmation:

_____

_____

A DAY WITHOUT *laughter* IS A DAY WASTED

Date: _____ Wake-Up Time Today: _____ Hours of Sleep I Got Last Night: _____

My Mood: Morning   Afternoon   Evening

Food/Beverages I Had Today:

B _____

L _____

D _____

Snacks _____

_____

What I Did for Exercise Today: **My Water Intake:**

_____

_____

_____

_____

Did I feel any of the following today?:

- ☐ Sadness and/or crying
- ☐ Hopeless
- ☐ No energy/fatigue/lethargy
- ☐ Difficulty concentrating/making decisions
- ☐ Appetite is increased or decreased
- ☐ Lack of motivation
- ☐ Anger/frustration
- ☐ Lack of interest in activities I normally enjoy

What caused me to feel negative emotions today?

_____

_____

_____

_____

Go to your doctor/medical professional immediately if you are suicidal or your mood is not getting better.

Is there anything that I could have done to improve my day?

_____

_____

_____

_____

_____

Positive things that happened today:

_____

_____

_____

_____

_____

Today, I am grateful for:

_____

_____

_____

Goals/things I can do to make tomorrow better:

_____

_____

_____

Positive Affirmation:

_____

_____

_____

The greater the **+ STORM +** *the brighter the* **RAINBOW**

More of My Thoughts

My Favorite Positive Affirmations

Choose joy

Date: _____ Wake-Up Time Today: _____ Hours of Sleep I Got Last Night: _____

My Mood: Morning   Afternoon   Evening

😊 😐 😣 😠   😊 😐 😣 😠   😊 😐 😣 😠

Food/Beverages I Had Today: **What I Did for Exercise Today:**   **My Water Intake:**

B _____   _____

L _____   _____

D _____   _____

Snacks _____   _____

_____

Did I feel any of the following today?:   **What caused me to feel negative emotions today?**

☐ Sadness and/or crying   _____
☐ Hopeless
☐ No energy/fatigue/lethargy   _____
☐ Difficulty concentrating/making decisions
☐ Appetite is increased or decreased   _____
☐ Lack of motivation
☐ Anger/frustration
☐ Lack of interest in activities I normally enjoy   **Go to your doctor/medical immediately if you are suicidal or your mood is not getting better.**

Is there anything that I could have done to improve my day?   **Positive things that happened today:**

_____   _____

_____   _____

_____   _____

_____   _____

_____   _____

Today, I am grateful for: **Goals/things I can do to make tomorrow better:**

_____   _____

_____   _____

_____   _____

_____   _____

Positive Affirmation:

_____

_____   *One day at a time*

_____

Date: _____   Wake-Up Time Today: _____   Hours of Sleep I Got Last Night: _____

My Mood: Morning   Afternoon   Evening

Food/Beverages I Had Today: **What I Did for Exercise Today:**   **My Water Intake:**

B _____   _____

L _____   _____

D _____   _____

Snacks _____   _____

_____

Did I feel any of the following today?:   **What caused me to feel negative emotions today?**

☐ Sadness and/or crying   _____
☐ Hopeless
☐ No energy/fatigue/lethargy   _____
☐ Difficulty concentrating/making decisions
☐ Appetite is increased or decreased   _____
☐ Lack of motivation
☐ Anger/frustration   _____
☐ Lack of interest in activities I normally enjoy

                                            **Go to your doctor/medical professional
                                            immediately if you are suicidal or your mood is not
                                            getting better.**

Is there anything that I could have done to   **Positive things that happened today:
improve my day?**

_____   _____

_____   _____

_____   _____

_____   _____

_____   _____

Today, I am grateful for: **Goals/things I can do to make tomorrow better:**

_____   _____

_____   _____

_____   _____

Positive Affirmation:
_____

_____

_____

LIFE IS TOUGH
BUT
so
ARE YOU

Date: _____   Wake-Up Time Today: _____   Hours of Sleep I Got Last Night: _____

My Mood: Morning   Afternoon   Evening

What I Did for Exercise Today: **My Water Intake:**

B _____
      Food/Beverages I Had Today:
L _____

D _____

Snacks _____

_____

Did I feel any of the following today?:

☐ Sadness and/or crying
☐ Hopeless
☐ No energy/fatigue/lethargy
☐ Difficulty concentrating/making decisions
☐ Appetite is increased or decreased
☐ Lack of motivation
☐ Anger/frustration
☐ Lack of interest in activities I normally enjoy

What caused me to feel negative emotions today?

_____

_____

_____

Go to your doctor/medical professional immediately if you are suicidal or your mood is not getting better.

Is there anything that I could have done to improve my day?

_____
_____
_____
_____
_____

Positive things that happened today:

_____
_____
_____
_____

Today, I am grateful for:

_____
_____
_____

Goals/things I can do to make tomorrow better:

_____
_____
_____

Positive Affirmation:

_____
_____

you GOT this

Date: _____ Wake-Up Time Today: _____ Hours of Sleep I Got Last Night: _____

My Mood: Morning   Afternoon   Evening

Food/Beverages I Had Today: **What I Did for Exercise Today:** **My Water Intake:**

B _____   _____

L _____   _____

D _____   _____

Snacks _____   _____

_____

Did I feel any of the following today?:   **What caused me to feel negative emotions today?**

☐ Sadness and/or crying   _____

☐ Hopeless   _____

☐ No energy/fatigue/lethargy   _____

☐ Difficulty concentrating/making decisions   _____

☐ Appetite is increased or decreased

☐ Lack of motivation   ****Go to your doctor/medical professional

☐ Anger/frustration   immediately if you are suicidal or your mood is not

☐ Lack of interest in activities I normally enjoy   getting better.****

Is there anything that I could have done to improve my day?   **Positive things that happened today:**

_____   _____

_____   _____

_____   _____

_____   _____

_____   _____

Today, I am grateful for: **Goals/things I can do to make tomorrow better:**

_____   _____

_____   _____

_____   _____

_____   _____

Positive Affirmation:

_____   Choose

_____   joy

_____

Date: _____   Wake-Up Time Today: _____   Hours of Sleep I Got Last Night: _____

My Mood: Morning   Afternoon   Evening

Food/Beverages I Had Today: **What I Did for Exercise Today:**   **My Water Intake:**

B _____   _____

L _____   _____

D _____   _____

Snacks _____

_____

Did I feel any of the following today?:   **What caused me to feel negative emotions today?**

- ☐ Sadness and/or crying   _____
- ☐ Hopeless   _____
- ☐ No energy/fatigue/lethargy   _____
- ☐ Difficulty concentrating/making decisions   _____
- ☐ Appetite is increased or decreased
- ☐ Lack of motivation   ****Go to your doctor/medical professional
- ☐ Anger/frustration   immediately if you are suicidal or your mood is not
- ☐ Lack of interest in activities I normally enjoy   getting better.****

Is there anything that I could have done to improve my day?   **Positive things that happened today:**

_____   _____

_____   _____

_____   _____

_____   _____

Today, I am grateful for: **Goals/things I can do to make tomorrow better:**

_____   _____

_____   _____

_____   _____

Positive Affirmation: Every DAY IS A NEW beginning

_____

_____

Date: _____ Wake-Up Time Today: _____ Hours of Sleep I Got Last Night: _____

My Mood: Morning   Afternoon   Evening

Food/Beverages I Had Today: **What I Did for Exercise Today:**   **My Water Intake:**

B _____   _____

L _____   _____

D _____   _____

Snacks _____   _____

_____   _____

Did I feel any of the following today?:   **What caused me to feel negative emotions today?**

- ☐ Sadness and/or crying
- ☐ Hopeless
- ☐ No energy/fatigue/lethargy
- ☐ Difficulty concentrating/making decisions
- ☐ Appetite is increased or decreased
- ☐ Lack of motivation
- ☐ Anger/frustration
- ☐ Lack of interest in activities I normally enjoy

_____

_____

_____

_____

Go to your doctor/medical professional immediately if you are suicidal or your mood is not getting better.

Is there anything that I could have done to improve my day?   **Positive things that happened today:**

_____   _____

_____   _____

_____   _____

_____   _____

_____   _____

Today, I am grateful for: **Goals/things I can do to make tomorrow better:**

_____   _____

_____   _____

_____   _____

_____   _____

Positive Affirmation:

_____

_____

_____

A DAY WITHOUT *laughter* IS A DAY WASTED

Date: _____   Wake-Up Time Today: _____   Hours of Sleep I Got Last Night: _____

My Mood: Morning   Afternoon   Evening

Food/Beverages I Had Today: **What I Did for Exercise Today:**   **My Water Intake:**

B   _____   _____

L   _____   _____

D   _____   _____

Snacks _____   _____

_____   _____

Did I feel any of the following today?:   **What caused me to feel negative emotions today?**

- ☐ Sadness and/or crying   _____
- ☐ Hopeless   _____
- ☐ No energy/fatigue/lethargy   _____
- ☐ Difficulty concentrating/making decisions   _____
- ☐ Appetite is increased or decreased
- ☐ Lack of motivation   **Go to your doctor/medical professional
- ☐ Anger/frustration   immediately if you are suicidal or your mood is not
- ☐ Lack of interest in activities I normally enjoy getting better.****

Is there anything that I could have done to improve my day?   **Positive things that happened today:**

_____   _____

_____   _____

_____   _____

_____   _____

Today, I am grateful for: **Goals/things I can do to make tomorrow better:**

_____   _____

_____   _____

_____   _____

Positive Affirmation: _____

_____

The greater the
★ STORM ★
the brighter the
RAINBOW

More of My Thoughts

My Positive Affirmations

Date: _____   Wake-Up Time Today: _____   Hours of Sleep I Got Last Night: _____

My Mood: Morning   Afternoon   Evening

Food/Beverages I Had Today:

B _____

L _____

D _____

Snacks _____

_____

What I Did for Exercise Today: **My Water Intake:**

_____

_____

_____

Did I feel any of the following today?:

- ☐ Sadness and/or crying
- ☐ Hopeless
- ☐ No energy/fatigue/lethargy
- ☐ Difficulty concentrating/making decisions
- ☐ Appetite is increased or decreased
- ☐ Lack of motivation
- ☐ Anger/frustration
- ☐ Lack of interest in activities I normally enjoy

What caused me to feel negative emotions today?

_____

_____

_____

Go to your doctor/medical professional immediately if you are suicidal or your mood is not getting better.

Is there anything that I could have done to improve my day?

_____

_____

_____

_____

_____

Positive things that happened today:

_____

_____

_____

_____

_____

Today, I am grateful for:

_____

_____

_____

Goals/things I can do to make tomorrow better:

_____

_____

_____

Positive Affirmation:

_____

_____

_____

One day at a time

Date: _____   Wake-Up Time Today: _____   Hours of Sleep I Got Last Night: _____

My Mood: Morning   Afternoon   Evening

Food/Beverages I Had Today: **What I Did for Exercise Today:**   **My Water Intake:**

B _____   _____

L _____   _____

D _____   _____

Snacks _____

_____

Did I feel any of the following today?:   **What caused me to feel negative emotions today?**

☐ Sadness and/or crying   _____
☐ Hopeless
☐ No energy/fatigue/lethargy   _____
☐ Difficulty concentrating/making decisions
☐ Appetite is increased or decreased   _____
☐ Lack of motivation
☐ Anger/frustration   **Go to your doctor/medical professional
☐ Lack of interest in activities I normally enjoy   immediately if you are suicidal or your mood is not
                                            getting better.**

Is there anything that I could have done to   **Positive things that happened today:**
improve my day?

_____   _____

_____   _____

_____   _____

_____   _____

_____   _____

Today, I am grateful for: **Goals/things I can do to make tomorrow better:**

_____   _____

_____   _____

_____   _____

Positive Affirmation:

_____

_____

LIFE IS TOUGH
BUT
SO
ARE YOU

Date: _____ Wake-Up Time Today: _____ Hours of Sleep I Got Last Night: _____

My Mood: Morning   Afternoon   Evening

What I Did for Exercise Today: My Water Intake:

B _____
Food/Beverages I Had Today:
L _____
D _____
Snacks _____
_____

Did I feel any of the following today?:

- ☐ Sadness and/or crying
- ☐ Hopeless
- ☐ No energy/fatigue/lethargy
- ☐ Difficulty concentrating/making decisions
- ☐ Appetite is increased or decreased
- ☐ Lack of motivation
- ☐ Anger/frustration
- ☐ Lack of interest in activities I normally enjoy

What caused me to feel negative emotions today?

_____
_____
_____

Go to your doctor/medical professional immediately if you are suicidal or your mood is not getting better.

Is there anything that I could have done to improve my day?

_____
_____
_____
_____
_____

Positive things that happened today:

_____
_____
_____
_____
_____

Today, I am grateful for:

_____
_____
_____
_____

Goals/things I can do to make tomorrow better:

_____
_____
_____
_____

Positive Affirmation:

_____
_____
_____
_____

you GOT this

Date: _____   Wake-Up Time Today: _____   Hours of Sleep I Got Last Night: _____

My Mood: Morning   Afternoon   Evening

Food/Beverages I Had Today:

B _____

L _____

D _____

Snacks _____

_____

What I Did for Exercise Today: **My Water Intake:**

_____

_____

_____

_____

Did I feel any of the following today?:

☐ Sadness and/or crying
☐ Hopeless
☐ No energy/fatigue/lethargy
☐ Difficulty concentrating/making decisions
☐ Appetite is increased or decreased
☐ Lack of motivation
☐ Anger/frustration
☐ Lack of interest in activities I normally enjoy

What caused me to feel negative emotions today?

_____

_____

_____

_____

Go to your doctor/medical professional immediately if you are suicidal or your mood is not getting better.

Is there anything that I could have done to improve my day?

_____

_____

_____

_____

_____

Positive things that happened today:

_____

_____

_____

_____

Today, I am grateful for:

_____

_____

_____

_____

Goals/things I can do to make tomorrow better:

_____

_____

_____

_____

Positive Affirmation:

_____

_____

_____

Choose joy

Date: _____ Wake-Up Time Today: _____ Hours of Sleep I Got Last Night: _____

My Mood: Morning   Afternoon   Evening

Food/Beverages I Had Today:

B _____

L _____

D _____

Snacks _____

_____

What I Did for Exercise Today: **My Water Intake:**

_____

_____

Did I feel any of the following today?:

- ☐ Sadness and/or crying
- ☐ Hopeless
- ☐ No energy/fatigue/lethargy
- ☐ Difficulty concentrating/making decisions
- ☐ Appetite is increased or decreased
- ☐ Lack of motivation
- ☐ Anger/frustration
- ☐ Lack of interest in activities I normally enjoy

What caused me to feel negative emotions today?

_____

_____

_____

Go to your doctor/medical professional immediately if you are suicidal or your mood is not getting better.

Is there anything that I could have done to improve my day?

_____
_____
_____
_____
_____

Positive things that happened today:

_____
_____
_____
_____
_____

Today, I am grateful for:

_____
_____
_____

Goals/things I can do to make tomorrow better:

_____
_____
_____

Positive Affirmation:

_____
_____
_____

Every DAY IS A NEW beginning

Date: _____ Wake-Up Time Today: _____ Hours of Sleep I Got Last Night: _____

My Mood: Morning Afternoon Evening

Food/Beverages I Had Today: What I Did for Exercise Today: My Water Intake:

B _____   _____

L _____   _____

D _____   _____

Snacks _____

_____

Did I feel any of the following today?:

☐ Sadness and/or crying
☐ Hopeless
☐ No energy/fatigue/lethargy
☐ Difficulty concentrating/making decisions
☐ Appetite is increased or decreased
☐ Lack of motivation
☐ Anger/frustration
☐ Lack of interest in activities I normally enjoy

What caused me to feel negative emotions today?

_____

_____

_____

Go to your doctor/medical professional immediately if you are suicidal or your mood is not getting better.

Is there anything that I could have done to improve my day?

_____

_____

_____

_____

_____

Positive things that happened today:

_____

_____

_____

_____

_____

Today, I am grateful for:

_____

_____

_____

Goals/things I can do to make tomorrow better:

_____

_____

_____

Positive Affirmation:

_____

_____

A DAY WITHOUT *laughter* IS A DAY WASTED

Date: _____   Wake-Up Time Today: _____   Hours of Sleep I Got Last Night: _____

My Mood: Morning   Afternoon   Evening

Food/Beverages I Had Today: **What I Did for Exercise Today:**   **My Water Intake:**

B _____   _____

L _____   _____

D _____   _____

Snacks _____   _____

_____

Did I feel any of the following today?:   **What caused me to feel negative emotions today?**

- ☐ Sadness and/or crying   _____
- ☐ Hopeless
- ☐ No energy/fatigue/lethargy   _____
- ☐ Difficulty concentrating/making decisions
- ☐ Appetite is increased or decreased   _____
- ☐ Lack of motivation
- ☐ Anger/frustration   ****Go to your doctor/medical professional
- ☐ Lack of interest in activities I normally enjoy   immediately if you are suicidal or your mood is not
                                               getting better.****

Is there anything that I could have done to   **Positive things that happened today:**
improve my day?

_____   _____

_____   _____

_____   _____

_____   _____

_____   _____

Today, I am grateful for: **Goals/things I can do to make tomorrow better:**

_____   _____

_____   _____

_____   _____

_____   _____

Positive Affirmation: _____

_____   *The greater the*
                                               ✦ STORM ✦
_____   *the brighter the*
                                               RAINBOW

More of My Thoughts

My Favorite Positive Affirmations

Love
Yourself

Date: _____ Wake-Up Time Today: _____ Hours of Sleep I Got Last Night: _____

My Mood: Morning   Afternoon   Evening

Food/Beverages I Had Today:

What I Did for Exercise Today: **My Water Intake:**

B _____

L _____

D _____   _____

Snacks _____   _____

_____

Did I feel any of the following today?:

- ☐ Sadness and/or crying
- ☐ Hopeless
- ☐ No energy/fatigue/lethargy
- ☐ Difficulty concentrating/making decisions
- ☐ Appetite is increased or decreased
- ☐ Lack of motivation
- ☐ Anger/frustration
- ☐ Lack of interest in activities I normally enjoy

What caused me to feel negative emotions today?

_____

_____

_____

_____

Go to your doctor/medical professional immediately if you are suicidal or your mood is not getting better.

Is there anything that I could have done to improve my day?

_____

_____

_____

_____

_____

Positive things that happened today:

_____

_____

_____

_____

_____

Today, I am grateful for:

_____

_____

_____

Goals/things I can do to make tomorrow better:

_____

_____

_____

Positive Affirmation:

_____

_____

One day at a time

Date: _____ Wake-Up Time Today: _____ Hours of Sleep I Got Last Night: _____

My Mood: Morning   Afternoon   Evening

Food/Beverages I Had Today: **What I Did for Exercise Today:**   **My Water Intake:**

B _____   _____

L _____   _____

D _____   _____

Snacks _____

_____

Did I feel any of the following today?:   **What caused me to feel negative emotions today?**

☐ Sadness and/or crying   _____
☐ Hopeless
☐ No energy/fatigue/lethargy   _____
☐ Difficulty concentrating/making decisions
☐ Appetite is increased or decreased   _____
☐ Lack of motivation
☐ Anger/frustration   ****Go to your doctor/medical professional
☐ Lack of interest in activities I normally enjoy   immediately if you are suicidal or your mood is not
                                            getting better.****

Is there anything that I could have done to   **Positive things that happened today:
improve my day?**

_____   _____

_____   _____

_____   _____

_____   _____

_____   _____

Today, I am grateful for: **Goals/things I can do to make tomorrow better:**

_____   _____

_____   _____

_____   _____

_____   _____

Positive Affirmation:

_____

_____   LIFE IS TOUGH
                                                                          ★★★ BUT ★★★
_____   so
                                                                          ARE YOU

Date: _____ Wake-Up Time Today: _____ Hours of Sleep I Got Last Night: _____

My Mood: Morning   Afternoon   Evening

What I Did for Exercise Today: **My Water Intake:**

B _____
            Food/Beverages I Had Today: _____

L _____

D _____

Snacks _____

_____

Did I feel any of the following today?:

- ☐ Sadness and/or crying
- ☐ Hopeless
- ☐ No energy/fatigue/lethargy
- ☐ Difficulty concentrating/making decisions
- ☐ Appetite is increased or decreased
- ☐ Lack of motivation
- ☐ Anger/frustration
- ☐ Lack of interest in activities I normally enjoy

What caused me to feel negative emotions today?

_____

_____

_____

Go to your doctor/medical professional immediately if you are suicidal or your mood is not getting better.

Is there anything that I could have done to improve my day?

_____

_____

_____

_____

Positive things that happened today:

_____

_____

_____

_____

Today, I am grateful for:

_____

_____

_____

_____

Goals/things I can do to make tomorrow better:

_____

_____

_____

_____

Positive Affirmation:

_____

_____

_____

you GOT this

Date: _____ Wake-Up Time Today: _____ Hours of Sleep I Got Last Night: _____

My Mood: Morning   Afternoon   Evening

Food/Beverages I Had Today: **What I Did for Exercise Today:**   **My Water Intake:**

B _____   _____

L _____   _____

D _____   _____

Snacks _____   _____

_____

Did I feel any of the following today?:

- ☐ Sadness and/or crying
- ☐ Hopeless
- ☐ No energy/fatigue/lethargy
- ☐ Difficulty concentrating/making decisions
- ☐ Appetite is increased or decreased
- ☐ Lack of motivation
- ☐ Anger/frustration
- ☐ Lack of interest in activities I normally enjoy

What caused me to feel negative emotions today?

_____

_____

_____

Go to your doctor/medical professional immediately if you are suicidal or your mood is not getting better.

Is there anything that I could have done to improve my day?

_____

_____

_____

_____

_____

Positive things that happened today:

_____

_____

_____

_____

_____

Today, I am grateful for:

_____

_____

_____

Goals/things I can do to make tomorrow better:

_____

_____

_____

Positive Affirmation:

_____

_____

_____

Choose joy

Date: _____ Wake-Up Time Today: _____ Hours of Sleep I Got Last Night: _____

My Mood: Morning   Afternoon   Evening

Food/Beverages I Had Today: **What I Did for Exercise Today:**   **My Water Intake:**

B _____   _____

L _____   _____

D _____   _____

Snacks _____

_____   _____

Did I feel any of the following today?:   **What caused me to feel negative emotions today?**

- ☐ Sadness and/or crying
- ☐ Hopeless   _____
- ☐ No energy/fatigue/lethargy   _____
- ☐ Difficulty concentrating/making decisions   _____
- ☐ Appetite is increased or decreased
- ☐ Lack of motivation
- ☐ Anger/frustration   ****Go to your doctor/medical professional
- ☐ Lack of interest in activities I normally enjoy   immediately if you are suicidal or your mood is not
                                                   getting better.****

**Is there anything that I could have done to
improve my day?**   **Positive things that happened today:**

_____   _____

_____   _____

_____   _____

_____   _____

_____   _____

Today, I am grateful for: **Goals/things I can do to make tomorrow better:**

_____   _____

_____   _____

_____   _____

Positive Affirmation:

_____

_____   Every DAY IS A New beginning

Date: _____   Wake-Up Time Today: _____   Hours of Sleep I Got Last Night: _____

My Mood: Morning   Afternoon   Evening

Food/Beverages I Had Today: **What I Did for Exercise Today:**   **My Water Intake:**

B _____   _____

L _____   _____

D _____   _____

Snacks _____   _____

_____   _____

Did I feel any of the following today?:   **What caused me to feel negative emotions today?**

☐   Sadness and/or crying   _____
☐   Hopeless
☐   No energy/fatigue/lethargy   _____
☐   Difficulty concentrating/making decisions
☐   Appetite is increased or decreased   _____
☐   Lack of motivation
☐   Anger/frustration   _____
☐   Lack of interest in activities I normally enjoy

Go to your doctor/medical professional immediately if you are suicidal or your mood is not getting better.

Is there anything that I could have done to improve my day?   **Positive things that happened today:**

_____   _____

_____   _____

_____   _____

_____   _____

_____   _____

Today, I am grateful for: **Goals/things I can do to make tomorrow better:**

_____   _____

_____   _____

_____   _____

_____   _____

Positive Affirmation:
_____

_____

_____

A DAY WITHOUT *laughter* IS A DAY WASTED

Date: _____ Wake-Up Time Today: _____ Hours of Sleep I Got Last Night: _____

My Mood: Morning   Afternoon   Evening

Food/Beverages I Had Today: **What I Did for Exercise Today:**   **My Water Intake:**

B _____   _____

L _____   _____

D _____   _____

Snacks _____   _____

_____

Did I feel any of the following today?:   **What caused me to feel negative emotions today?**

☐ Sadness and/or crying   _____
☐ Hopeless   _____
☐ No energy/fatigue/lethargy   _____
☐ Difficulty concentrating/making decisions   _____
☐ Appetite is increased or decreased
☐ Lack of motivation   ****Go to your doctor/medical professional
☐ Anger/frustration   immediately if you are suicidal or your mood is not
☐ Lack of interest in activities I normally enjoy   getting better.****

Is there anything that I could have done to   Positive things that happened today:
improve my day?

_____   _____

_____   _____

_____   _____

_____   _____

Today, I am grateful for: **Goals/things I can do to make tomorrow better:**

_____   _____

_____   _____

_____   _____

Positive Affirmation: _____

_____

The greater the
✦ STORM ✦
the brighter the
RAINBOW

More of My Thoughts

My Positive Affirmations

Where there
IS
faith
THERE IS
· hope ·

Date: _____   Wake-Up Time Today: _____   Hours of Sleep I Got Last Night: _____

My Mood: Morning   Afternoon   Evening

😊 😐 😣 😠   😊 😐 😣 😠   😊 😐 😣 😠

Food/Beverages I Had Today: **What I Did for Exercise Today:**   **My Water Intake:**

B _____   _____

L _____   _____

D _____   _____

Snacks _____   _____

_____   _____

Did I feel any of the following today?:   **What caused me to feel negative emotions today?**

☐ Sadness and/or crying   _____
☐ Hopeless   _____
☐ No energy/fatigue/lethargy   _____
☐ Difficulty concentrating/making decisions   _____
☐ Appetite is increased or decreased
☐ Lack of motivation   ****Go to your doctor/medical professional
☐ Anger/frustration   immediately if you are suicidal or your mood is not
☐ Lack of interest in activities I normally enjoy   getting better.****

Is there anything that I could have done to   **Positive things that happened today:**
improve my day?

_____   _____

_____   _____

_____   _____

_____   _____

_____   _____

Today, I am grateful for: **Goals/things I can do to make tomorrow better:**

_____   _____

_____   _____

_____   _____

_____   _____

Positive Affirmation:

_____

_____   *One day at a time*

_____

Date: _____ Wake-Up Time Today: _____ Hours of Sleep I Got Last Night: _____

My Mood: Morning   Afternoon   Evening

Food/Beverages I Had Today: **What I Did for Exercise Today:**   **My Water Intake:**

B _____   _____

L _____   _____

D _____   _____

Snacks _____   _____

_____

Did I feel any of the following today?:   **What caused me to feel negative emotions today?**

☐ Sadness and/or crying   _____
☐ Hopeless
☐ No energy/fatigue/lethargy   _____
☐ Difficulty concentrating/making decisions
☐ Appetite is increased or decreased   _____
☐ Lack of motivation
☐ Anger/frustration   _____
☐ Lack of interest in activities I normally enjoy

**Is there anything that I could have done to   **Go to your doctor/medical professional
improve my day?**   immediately if you are suicidal or your mood is not
                                             getting better.**

                                             Positive things that happened today:

_____   _____

_____   _____

_____   _____

_____   _____

Today, I am grateful for: **Goals/things I can do to make tomorrow better:**

_____   _____

_____   _____

_____   _____

Positive Affirmation:

_____

_____

LIFE IS TOUGH
★★★ BUT ★★★
so
ARE YOU

Date: _____ Wake-Up Time Today: _____ Hours of Sleep I Got Last Night: _____

My Mood: Morning   Afternoon   Evening

What I Did for Exercise Today: **My Water Intake:**

B _____
Food/Beverages I Had Today: _____
L _____
D _____   _____
Snacks _____
_____

Did I feel any of the following today?:

☐ Sadness and/or crying
☐ Hopeless
☐ No energy/fatigue/lethargy
☐ Difficulty concentrating/making decisions
☐ Appetite is increased or decreased
☐ Lack of motivation
☐ Anger/frustration
☐ Lack of interest in activities I normally enjoy

What caused me to feel negative emotions today?

_____
_____
_____
_____

Go to your doctor/medical professional immediately if you are suicidal or your mood is not getting better.

Is there anything that I could have done to improve my day?

_____
_____
_____
_____
_____

Positive things that happened today:

_____
_____
_____
_____
_____

Today, I am grateful for:

_____
_____
_____
_____

Goals/things I can do to make tomorrow better:

_____
_____
_____
_____

Positive Affirmation:

_____
_____
_____

you GOT this

Date: _____ Wake-Up Time Today: _____ Hours of Sleep I Got Last Night: _____

My Mood: Morning   Afternoon   Evening

Food/Beverages I Had Today: **What I Did for Exercise Today:**   **My Water Intake:**

B _____   _____

L _____   _____

D _____   _____

Snacks _____   _____

_____

Did I feel any of the following today?:   **What caused me to feel negative emotions today?**

- ☐ Sadness and/or crying
- ☐ Hopeless
- ☐ No energy/fatigue/lethargy
- ☐ Difficulty concentrating/making decisions
- ☐ Appetite is increased or decreased
- ☐ Lack of motivation
- ☐ Anger/frustration
- ☐ Lack of interest in activities I normally enjoy

_____

_____

_____

Go to your doctor/medical professional immediately if you are suicidal or your mood is not getting better.

Is there anything that I could have done to improve my day?   **Positive things that happened today:**

_____   _____

_____   _____

_____   _____

_____   _____

Today, I am grateful for: **Goals/things I can do to make tomorrow better:**

_____   _____

_____   _____

_____   _____

Positive Affirmation:

_____

_____

Choose joy

Date: _____ Wake-Up Time Today: _____ Hours of Sleep I Got Last Night: _____

My Mood: Morning   Afternoon   Evening

😊 😐 😣 😠   😊 😐 😣 😠   😊 😐 😣 😠

Food/Beverages I Had Today: **What I Did for Exercise Today:**   **My Water Intake:**

B _____   _____

L _____   _____

D _____   _____

Snacks _____   _____

_____   _____

Did I feel any of the following today?:

- ☐ Sadness and/or crying
- ☐ Hopeless
- ☐ No energy/fatigue/lethargy
- ☐ Difficulty concentrating/making decisions
- ☐ Appetite is increased or decreased
- ☐ Lack of motivation
- ☐ Anger/frustration
- ☐ Lack of interest in activities I normally enjoy

What caused me to feel negative emotions today?

_____

_____

_____

Go to your doctor/medical professional immediately if you are suicidal or your mood is not getting better.

Is there anything that I could have done to improve my day?

_____

_____

_____

_____

_____

Positive things that happened today:

_____

_____

_____

_____

_____

Today, I am grateful for:

_____

_____

_____

_____

Goals/things I can do to make tomorrow better:

_____

_____

_____

Positive Affirmation:

_____

_____

_____

Every DAY IS A NEW beginning

Date: _____   Wake-Up Time Today: _____   Hours of Sleep I Got Last Night: _____

My Mood: Morning   Afternoon   Evening

Food/Beverages I Had Today: **What I Did for Exercise Today:**   **My Water Intake:**

B   _____   _____

L   _____   _____

D   _____   _____

Snacks _____   _____

_____

Did I feel any of the following today?:   **What caused me to feel negative emotions today?**

- ☐ Sadness and/or crying   _____
- ☐ Hopeless
- ☐ No energy/fatigue/lethargy   _____
- ☐ Difficulty concentrating/making decisions   _____
- ☐ Appetite is increased or decreased
- ☐ Lack of motivation
- ☐ Anger/frustration   ****Go to your doctor/medical professional
- ☐ Lack of interest in activities I normally enjoy   immediately if you are suicidal or your mood is not
                                                              getting better.****

Is there anything that I could have done to   **Positive things that happened today:**
improve my day?

_____   _____

_____   _____

_____   _____

_____   _____

Today, I am grateful for: **Goals/things I can do to make tomorrow better:**

_____   _____

_____   _____

_____   _____

Positive Affirmation: _____

_____

_____

A DAY WITHOUT
laughter
IS A DAY WASTED

Date: _____ Wake-Up Time Today: _____ Hours of Sleep I Got Last Night: _____

My Mood: Morning   Afternoon   Evening

Food/Beverages I Had Today: **What I Did for Exercise Today:**   **My Water Intake:**

B _____

L _____

D _____

Snacks _____

_____

Did I feel any of the following today?:

- ☐ Sadness and/or crying
- ☐ Hopeless
- ☐ No energy/fatigue/lethargy
- ☐ Difficulty concentrating/making decisions
- ☐ Appetite is increased or decreased
- ☐ Lack of motivation
- ☐ Anger/frustration
- ☐ Lack of interest in activities I normally enjoy

What caused me to feel negative emotions today?

_____

_____

_____

_____

Go to your doctor/medical professional immediately if you are suicidal or your mood is not getting better.

Is there anything that I could have done to improve my day?

_____

_____

_____

_____

Positive things that happened today:

_____

_____

_____

_____

Today, I am grateful for:

_____

_____

_____

Goals/things I can do to make tomorrow better:

_____

_____

_____

Positive Affirmation:

_____

_____

_____

The greater the
✦ STORM ✦
the brighter the
RAINBOW

My Favorite Positive Affirmations

Create Your Own HAPPINESS

HAPPY

Date: _____   Wake-Up Time Today: _____   Hours of Sleep I Got Last Night: _____

My Mood: Morning   Afternoon   Evening

😊 😐 😖 😠   😊 😐 😖 😠   😊 😐 😖 😠

Food/Beverages I Had Today: **What I Did for Exercise Today:**   **My Water Intake:**

B _____   _____

L _____   _____

D _____   _____

Snacks _____   _____

_____   _____

Did I feel any of the following today?:   **What caused me to feel negative emotions today?**

- ☐ Sadness and/or crying   _____
- ☐ Hopeless   _____
- ☐ No energy/fatigue/lethargy   _____
- ☐ Difficulty concentrating/making decisions   _____
- ☐ Appetite is increased or decreased   _____
- ☐ Lack of motivation
- ☐ Anger/frustration   ****Go to your doctor/medical professional
- ☐ Lack of interest in activities I normally enjoy   immediately if you are suicidal or your mood is not
                                           getting better.****

Is there anything that I could have done to improve my day?   **Positive things that happened today:**

_____   _____

_____   _____

_____   _____

_____   _____

_____   _____

Today, I am grateful for: **Goals/things I can do to make tomorrow better:**

_____   _____

_____   _____

_____   _____

Positive Affirmation:

_____

_____

_____

One day at a time

Date: _____   Wake-Up Time Today: _____   Hours of Sleep I Got Last Night: _____

My Mood: Morning   Afternoon   Evening

Food/Beverages I Had Today: **What I Did for Exercise Today:**   **My Water Intake:**

B _____   _____

L _____   _____

D _____   _____

Snacks _____   _____

_____

Did I feel any of the following today?:   **What caused me to feel negative emotions today?**

☐ Sadness and/or crying   _____
☐ Hopeless
☐ No energy/fatigue/lethargy   _____
☐ Difficulty concentrating/making decisions
☐ Appetite is increased or decreased   _____
☐ Lack of motivation
☐ Anger/frustration   ****Go to your doctor/medical professional
☐ Lack of interest in activities I normally enjoy   immediately if you are suicidal or your mood is not
                                             getting better.****

Is there anything that I could have done to   Positive things that happened today:
improve my day?

_____   _____

_____   _____

_____   _____

_____   _____

_____   _____

Today, I am grateful for: **Goals/things I can do to make tomorrow better:**

_____   _____

_____   _____

_____   _____

Positive Affirmation:

_____

_____

_____

LIFE IS TOUGH
*** BUT ***
SO
ARE YOU

Date: _____   Wake-Up Time Today: _____   Hours of Sleep I Got Last Night: _____

My Mood: Morning   Afternoon   Evening

What I Did for Exercise Today: **My Water Intake:**

B _____

L _____   **Food/Beverages I Had Today:**

D _____

Snacks _____

_____

Did I feel any of the following today?:   **What caused me to feel negative emotions today?**

- ☐ Sadness and/or crying
- ☐ Hopeless
- ☐ No energy/fatigue/lethargy
- ☐ Difficulty concentrating/making decisions
- ☐ Appetite is increased or decreased
- ☐ Lack of motivation
- ☐ Anger/frustration
- ☐ Lack of interest in activities I normally enjoy

Go to your doctor/medical professional immediately if you are suicidal or your mood is not getting better.

Is there anything that I could have done to improve my day?

Positive things that happened today:

Today, I am grateful for:

Goals/things I can do to make tomorrow better:

Positive Affirmation:

you GOT this

Date: _____ Wake-Up Time Today: _____ Hours of Sleep I Got Last Night: _____

My Mood: Morning   Afternoon   Evening

Food/Beverages I Had Today: **What I Did for Exercise Today:**   **My Water Intake:**

B _____   _____

L _____   _____

D _____   _____

Snacks _____   _____

_____   _____

Did I feel any of the following today?:   **What caused me to feel negative emotions today?**

- ☐ Sadness and/or crying   _____
- ☐ Hopeless
- ☐ No energy/fatigue/lethargy   _____
- ☐ Difficulty concentrating/making decisions
- ☐ Appetite is increased or decreased   _____
- ☐ Lack of motivation
- ☐ Anger/frustration   ****Go to your doctor/medical professional
- ☐ Lack of interest in activities I normally enjoy   immediately if you are suicidal or your mood is not
                                               getting better.****

Is there anything that I could have done to improve my day?   **Positive things that happened today:**

_____   _____

_____   _____

_____   _____

_____   _____

Today, I am grateful for: **Goals/things I can do to make tomorrow better:**

_____   _____

_____   _____

_____   _____

Positive Affirmation:

_____   *Choose joy*

_____

Date: _____ Wake-Up Time Today: _____ Hours of Sleep I Got Last Night: _____

My Mood: Morning   Afternoon   Evening

Food/Beverages I Had Today:

                                                              What I Did for Exercise Today: **My Water Intake:**

B _____   _____

L _____   _____

D _____   _____

Snacks _____   _____

     _____

Did I feel any of the following today?:   **What caused me to feel negative emotions today?**

- ☐ Sadness and/or crying
- ☐ Hopeless
- ☐ No energy/fatigue/lethargy
- ☐ Difficulty concentrating/making decisions
- ☐ Appetite is increased or decreased
- ☐ Lack of motivation
- ☐ Anger/frustration
- ☐ Lack of interest in activities I normally enjoy

Go to your doctor/medical professional immediately if you are suicidal or your mood is not getting better.

Is there anything that I could have done to improve my day?   **Positive things that happened today:**

_____   _____

_____   _____

_____   _____

_____   _____

_____   _____

Today, I am grateful for: **Goals/things I can do to make tomorrow better:**

_____   _____

_____   _____

_____   _____

Positive Affirmation: _____

_____

_____

Every DAY IS A NEW beginning

Date: _____   Wake-Up Time Today: _____   Hours of Sleep I Got Last Night: _____

My Mood: Morning   Afternoon   Evening

Food/Beverages I Had Today: **What I Did for Exercise Today:**   **My Water Intake:**

B _____   _____

L _____   _____

D _____   _____

Snacks _____   _____

_____

Did I feel any of the following today?:   **What caused me to feel negative emotions today?**

☐ Sadness and/or crying   _____
☐ Hopeless
☐ No energy/fatigue/lethargy   _____
☐ Difficulty concentrating/making decisions
☐ Appetite is increased or decreased   _____
☐ Lack of motivation
☐ Anger/frustration   ****Go to your doctor/medical professional
☐ Lack of interest in activities I normally enjoy   immediately if you are suicidal or your mood is not
                                                           getting better.****

Is there anything that I could have done to   Positive things that happened today:
improve my day?

_____   _____

_____   _____

_____   _____

_____   _____

_____

Today, I am grateful for: **Goals/things I can do to make tomorrow better:**

_____   _____

_____   _____

_____   _____

Positive Affirmation: _____

_____   A DAY WITHOUT
_____   *laughter*
                                 IS A DAY WASTED

Date: _____   Wake-Up Time Today: _____   Hours of Sleep I Got Last Night: _____

My Mood: Morning   Afternoon   Evening

Food/Beverages I Had Today: **What I Did for Exercise Today:**   **My Water Intake:**

B   _____   _____

L   _____   _____

D   _____   _____

Snacks _____   _____

     _____

Did I feel any of the following today?:   **What caused me to feel negative emotions today?**

☐   Sadness and/or crying   _____
☐   Hopeless
☐   No energy/fatigue/lethargy   _____
☐   Difficulty concentrating/making decisions
☐   Appetite is increased or decreased   _____
☐   Lack of motivation
☐   Anger/frustration   **Go to your doctor/medical professional
☐   Lack of interest in activities I normally enjoy   immediately if you are suicidal or your mood is not
                                              getting better.**

Is there anything that I could have done to   **Positive things that happened today:
improve my day?**

_____   _____

_____   _____

_____   _____

_____   _____

_____   _____

Today, I am grateful for: **Goals/things I can do to make tomorrow better:**

_____   _____

_____   _____

_____   _____

Positive Affirmation:

_____   *The greater the*
                                           ✦ STORM ✦
_____   *the brighter the*
                                           RAINBOW
_____

Part Two

This part of the journal is where you can come whenever you need to plan your goals, doodle or draw what you're feeling. You can also color to de-stress.

don't just exist live

My Goals for a Healthier Mind, Body, & Soul

My Goals	Steps I need to Take to Reach My Goals	Date to Achieve My Goal (Be Specific)
To think more positively about situations	When my brain thinks of something negative, I need to stop the thought & replace it with a positive thought instead.	

My Goals for a Healthier Mind, Body, & Soul

My Goals	Steps I need to Take to Reach My Goals	Date to Achieve My Goal (Be Specific)

My Doodles

FIND YOUR
fire

My Doodles

Shoot for the MOON
FOR THE
and if you miss
YOU will still be AMONG
the stars

My Doodles

Sometimes You **Win** & Sometimes You **Learn**

My Doodles

DANCE *heart* WITH YOUR YOUR *feet* WILL FOLLOW

Am I Getting Enough Me Time?

Make a list of things that you enjoy doing & help to improve your mood. Keep track of how frequently you are doing things you like by using the checkboxes below.

	M	T	W	T	F	S	S
	☐	☐	☐	☐	☐	☐	☐
	☐	☐	☐	☐	☐	☐	☐
	☐	☐	☐	☐	☐	☐	☐
	☐	☐	☐	☐	☐	☐	☐
	☐	☐	☐	☐	☐	☐	☐
	☐	☐	☐	☐	☐	☐	☐
	☐	☐	☐	☐	☐	☐	☐
	☐	☐	☐	☐	☐	☐	☐
	☐	☐	☐	☐	☐	☐	☐
	☐	☐	☐	☐	☐	☐	☐
	☐	☐	☐	☐	☐	☐	☐

THANKFUL and Blessed

My Self Care Goals

Things I need to do more of for the health of my mind, body, and/or spirit:

How I can make the above things happen:

IT does NOT MATTER
HOW SLOWLY you GO
AS LONG as
YOU do NOT STOP

My Self Care Goals

Things I need to do more of for the health of my mind, body, and/or spirit:

How I can make the above things happen:

"Love yourself first, and everything else will fall into place." — Lucille Ball

A loving heart is the truest wisdom

~Charles Dickens~

See more of our journals at
https://www.CaptivatingJournals.com